T0160786

FIRE BREAK

GEORGE ALBON

NIGHTBOAT BOOKS
CALLICOON, NEW YORK

Versions of these poems have appeared in *lyric&*, *Melodeon*, *New American Writing*, *Tinfish*, *Hummingbird*, *Syllogism*, *Five Fingers Review*, *26*, *traverse*, *commonweal*, *Ur-Vox*, *Parthenon West Review*, and *Estuaire* (in French translation by Daniel Canty). My sincere thanks to the editors for their interest.

A special thank you to Stephen Motika, Peggy Honeywell, Margaret Tedesco, and Ed Gilbert.

ISBN: 978-1-937658-13-7

Cover art: *Red Hex*, 2012 (front); *Black Line Harmony*, 2012 (back) by Clare Rojas. Courtesy of the artist and Gallery Paule Anglim, San Francisco.

Design and typesetting by Margaret Tedesco
Text set in Apollo and Gill Sans

Cataloging-in-publication data is available
from the Library of Congress

Distributed by University Press of New England
One Court Street
Lebanon, NH 03766
www.upne.com

NIGHTBOAT BOOKS
Callicoon, New York
www.nightboat.org

FOR DENNIS MORIBE

FIRE BREAK

When they told the myth in the present tense
I looked around

I had things behind me all scattered walls
I fronted them

I started out, then I was fore,
a vertical applying,

watching broad shapes to find the inaugural
moment

and shapes were ahead but what did I
step from—

moving leg and arm, in something's middle
I found me

turning into right and wrong, supporting
my weight in a gesture

and the piece to be made a planted twig
under the tree-line,

through unlocatable reeds and tissues the call
stood in

with appearance it uttered circles, first
the windows rained, then

the world did, a sprig of mint
breaking through

that tasted like shade, bricks for house
were clear bales

so thought could be like patience,
me trying

for profile in the borderless playgrounds—
spoke exampling itself

when it goes round and round—
restless stones

to catch and match, and face
takes on

where levels could be set there,
the newcomers

head over road
still holding their tickets upright

■

A candle brings in
and a region meanders

A pivot wanting surface

A trend in the overland
refigured by what we
can mean with searchlight

a census underfoot
a whole note parried

A megaphoned whisper.

■

High blank
of just

"woke up"

a low
steady sound

—car engine

on—timbre not
dynamics

going through
foldings

across
the yards

■

No sooner written

flowers in the sun

than contended

But to clothe ourselves
and see our breath,
see indistinctly far
others' bright figures,

that I don't know
what occurs
in words, that
spring a weather shift
that will have
causation, that
is the just
fact.

■

Does the sky disrupt? I followed you, you were rapid, I followed you to seal it off. The horse's head grew long so that the eyes would rise above the grass line, to notice predators. The sidelong glance grew so inscrutable I really felt I was in another world. They seemed all live things with hearts in them. I need more time to patch in the last one, a signature in black crayon taking up the middle of the page. To hop in such a way that it would communicate to the local sparrows, subtitles at the grass line. Environs concealing that this is the United States, the "help" live here not affording the continent. I sought your knee during the premonition, its hairiness like horse nettle, comfort and alien. Such that a heat lag would also incarnate while it augured, a set-out on the recent forms, your full expression, my liquid fray.

Murmur-curl.

The sky disrupts.

■

To land in the dense
before called to motion.

A blanket or mat
on a host floor.

Tiny enlargements.
Monody cog-tick

where reclamation is
and the gaps are.

A submerged
tapestry emerges

into a day
evident only.

Before work, or ar-
resting sentence.

■

I look at your photo,
you in the painted
eucalyptus

The sky solid
blue, deepening
upward

You seem light-
hearted all throughout
the focus-burn

■

The eggs nudged into
the natural
rock enclosure,
away from the ledge—

skirt pockets holding
the truffles, fungus
as the feet root
further in.

This like others
at a crucible
kept for
remittance.

I hand my wooden
cubes (nosegay,
intervals, oasis)
to slippery receivers.

■

I had to wait to understand the spoken words—some fell below hearing range. The airport soft tunnels, obligations leaning into one another. A waiting lounge where envoys have set up more or less permanent camp. I will live for months in a rhetorical outpost, walking through doorless spaces. Electrical connectives pushed waves from a mounted box: half heard, half clarion, ears askew. The sun went behind and equalized all our tones, the directions were for everybody.

They looked out at the provisional capital.

One such explained to another why he stayed on, *it's pretty in the evening*.

■

Romanticism through the scientism
is what I hear

regularity of surround-space

he half-saws the limb
so that it *folds* allowing
him to get the upper branches which
are now near him upside down

I write between folds and revs

a star by a word
but I must've been distracted
I never wrote my addition

it broke with its covey
then settled back
in pattern hiding

Branch moving animist
until I see the tucked away
rope and man

■

In pictures, creatures were others' edges. Leaves were a fox, the fox was the shape of the space between the leaves: fox-shape from leaf-space. (Hare-shape from bush-and-hill.) (Badgers/knotholes, a tortoise/storm puddle.) It was a picture, it was a "world." The foreground was improbably well-stocked. In the try for balance the atoms of balance were lost. (There's just enough room for more raven.) (I can just make out the ears and snout.)

He held the book with both hands.

A picture is black and white. A design-picture.

Claws, as if grasping only the psychic space, a game's delayed promise. Soon there should be something that joins the corners to the depth of field, that can be felt with the fingers (and other muscles). Flexing, one releases the textures that will push one's native modulations *into* the land. Tramping on mast to reveal the open page, wherever it is in the house, in the forest, a blanket filled with soil, an anti-gravity set. There was a trail. There were little dots. One of them was a flower where it converged at the vanishing point.

Carefully, or rather, like an adult, he stepped through.

■

Pocket-
           unconscious,

inventing
under
           duress.

Quonset-hut-search.

Leaves on no seeded
land but a shore,

no ridge but information.

A teen writes It was a Life's work.

■

St. Brigid enlisted
to keep the progeny asleep

and myself peeking at the ways
you can exit a certain kind of package

Through the decades a "she" kept the slip
in a book with no print in it

My sense out of the package is a simple one
being that writing steadies itself toward the period

In his film the camera is street-pointed
never taking in even one degree of the sky

The refrigerator kicks on to my left, dull traffic
off the parkway on my right

Auditioners of the world
would consider this a warm bath

I give myself a ticket to claim,
that the impulses be in from the window

"The children of St. Brigid are willful and happy"
She kept the slip to read in her trials.

■

Rapid push of a stick,
haste in the design.

Another *what* is toppled.
The still-in-movement

makeweight of inertia,
time going to wet,

vision from the cutting.
Will tremble if the light

moves to sedentariness.
Then sighted on the return.

All around a cloud shell
to show us the stake.

■

Shout-voice to turn heads
on that two-streams

of foot traffic cirque
selling his Burn along

Terminal Market, woolen
cap in the ripping cold

    I read the sleeve, ask
    Are these your beats

■

Tending on the close side
the tried body capitulates

feeling to zero

a rushing eclipse, the night
runs across the lot

through the bedded rooms, your
care walking through

A prehensile glimpse
on the edge of eternity

calling for catching
Trouble-knot

Moved is led

■

Admitting, in erotic paces, and admission, as to the buildings. Both having to do with a conception of the sky. An inner ceiling, diaphanous but blunt, reaching over to get to touch. The mandate is to understand each other by facial imperative. With aquiline surface-readings we will fly over the cities, hands held in invisibility, using treetop contact as sensor. Below is the grid of living bound in time, a deaf lessening, made of concretes.

Here is a chunk of rock which you can see.

The substratum is filled out with new-moon

slate, a stick of chalk turned inside

out, as if to write recruiting verbs for a column's restless tenants. So much reading done standing up, looking forward. He didn't factor in plywood when he formulated the sky-book idea. Tilting the chunk so that the glitter tones appear in the same light. The other add-on, the star, is diminished, a field of rocks in a field outside the wall, in the rigors of this more interesting concentration. While airborne place the rock into your neighbor's free hand. Fieldborne, a different one will be felt in yours.

Activism, as of desire.

Relaxing, in the political.

■

To on our knees
face, closer
until touch

points

touch,
feeling of a
sudden coast

The pointing
finger's tip

Mark
of your under-
shirt still

tactual,
exhaling

neon-lit
corpoglyph.

■

My godmother the circle,

then I un-

twist the loops
to wash off the soap.

A cell planted in the yard
to appease the causes.

To do to be late, rush
of flood when I stand

Clockarrow suddenly parallel

The bath water
going out in
spirals.

■

A cloudy night cleared,
comet on path.

Tail like salt spilled on a table—
forward motion edging across a plane.

Parabolic one-shot not returning,
behavior crawling wind.

The movement closed, though arrival is ours.

■

SLOW in the road,
sunk across the width
of the lane. It
had become weathered.

What you wanted
to say you said
in those trains they have
against the syllable.

■

I hear a song-
ghost through what I
thought blank tape—

and the book
with smoke damage so

the words sit in
an added

brown frame—
if I keep

listening what
will I start to hear—
if I keep

reading will
the frame take over—

the frame, the song-ghost,

and my location, at
ten at night with
these veils.

■

The hand wave moves
to the side

the water wave
if you stand

will meet you at
different depths

then pull at you in
surging back

their sounds
are changing

the wind buzzing
through vinyl slats

smile a message
you have intercepted

message and uniform

■

Extensions into audition re: lack of sleep
turnoff to the settlement

Meeting animal eyes as it brings its head up
parked on the shoulder

Light of the coast which is a bundling blue haze
above blue water

Arches of the bridge set down in the ravine
not seen from cars

Boarded-up lodge past the gravel
groups gone out

Camera zooming back from the refugees
four on a couch

Talking head explains the nuances of policy
three-quarter profile

Tire tread lays pattern over the random footprint
The negotiation accordioned

■

Letter halting-
ly written, so it
was a signless hatch

so to try again

then wrote it as

if I were tracing it—

a tiny mistake but
jammed distance,
the paper's ground

and my cognition's
aerial view,

felt the sudden in

any action, all of them
a brush with something
in breathing at the room.

■

Water being is

what it fills

Action in that level
a force in it   not

ending with what I can't
see past, that is my limit

water fills the chasm
widens it

Capture the eon

where the plates forced
and a drop came out
and then there were cliff faces

In the insignificant midst
"be in nothing so moderate"

My limit a blessedness

the water goes out of sight

A sound commits it.

■

What I think of you
is in my skins.

Enclosing nerve
set, changing verb.

Moved and acted
past to now point.

Pressed in abandon.
Torso in yellow light.

Standing chest. The
there of you.

Beaded up on fore-
head, back of back

in the beginning
of literal skin.

To say my temperature
is also envelope.

One dry foot outside
the shower curtain.

I turn around.
I put my face around.

■

"I always use
Cremnitz white

when I paint

something alive,

it's always
a *code*

that it's alive."

I look at
the surface,

shine,

off the body.

The brink is large,

hard disc with cleft
open, a putative landmark
while the destination slips.

Exception as always, taken outside.

If turning the words around
to set them on the speaker
were mantle and laurel,
and nothing to fall off during the direction,
but a straight hit.

Not to gather the land between blinks.

Pilgrims are we. Ignited star chart.

Not swayed by the luck of the last.

■

for Daniel Davidson

At the ten thousandth mile
surrounded by
the deforest.

Entering this bowl . . .

The edges of possessive road . . .

It goes to the plain
so that being can take place.

Paper flowers commemorate
post-noon stretching the corners
to the extended visitor.

Yellow for waiting.

A cross where they went over.

■

Cirrus for stem
brushed up to
the stationary

cumulus
wind-current
brought

clearing into
visible forma-
tions

blip and roil
moving into
the area

■

A germ doesn't find,
doesn't see.
It sometimes spills.

Cirrus so
growing it
finally meshes

over.
I wait for you
to show up—

we'll go outside
town, behave
like germs.

I went over
to the accidental shelf

I found a statement
that called me in its curve.

This for that—
gift game weapon

Study of the vanished,
overtaken in intensities

Let melody stand for attachment.

Waking tracks in the sky, and the memory
parachutes into
disappearing.

Not to follow you

      task gone to ground
      shaky-resolved from life
      in the partitional times

but to ask *what*

rise

are you standing at

■

To write to place

an anniversary, however

false is
the calendar.

Stark of ledger, each
side a
tangle where it
pulls the skin off

Once he climbed
a tree while we fought for
points of what we
didn't understand in each other

Houses on the hills,
now I watch roads

the blandly serpentine arteries
blankminded from looking.

It happened.

It made a term.

Dendrobium blooms shoot
                                              out
at right
            angles

Lily of the
                    valley
(four corms) on the
                              register
Nameless music
                      nearby
a small force

The wrapped-up
                          surprise
on your
            person.

■

The embodied one
asks a crackle
Are you hungry

This barely kept-
over spectrum
of haunted
rationality

Live in a car, write
about your new
experiences by the light
of a cigarette lighter

and vibrations

stray and make
camp in the
assumptive
aftermath,

a close bone

strobing
moth tap

tone for
home.

—spikes of rain?
but it's

merely optical—
of looking

at pines
some ways
from one

another—
though the

non-optical
jostles.

■

Clipboard on my bed when I wake up
I touch a
    sheet of paper it sticks to my fingers
imagine walking through the floor trying
                   to unstick it
scraping noises inside and outside the house
I put the paper on the wall, start walking
               to the other wall
but as he says the invention of the
          other forms the I
other forms tempt me in my waking hours
not during sleeping
I live in a terranean world, I think about the
          following day in the current one
L's sessions in taxicabs were perhaps not
          his best
except as the architecture of Paris having an
        interior armature
Chris died two days ago, a year and a half life
             with lymphoma
My dream of him, lawn bag full of books, on the
         way to the library
after the postal clerk offered me a hearing test
still the paper sticking, I notice the feel on
    my fingers, four tips strangely engaged in
keeping it on
but to want to unstick also seems natural
so it's many sided nature I append
many sided

a regular weekend in the racing hills
I imagine a wet traction as they handbrake down
the Last Man pauses on "what is a star"
the coffeepot gurgles, then clicks
and the noise and sprawl of willed commerce will
                              be mine as soon as I
leave for work
in imitation "I used to be conciliatory,
          but now I am appropriate"
The returns of waves, the rote of labor
and the appearance of calm feeling followed by a vise

we'll plant a tree in the headlands, I'll read
                    sonnet 122
Thy gift, thy tables, are within my brain
Today is fogged in after weeks of sun
brown tips of the pine branches straight up like candles
like grasping the outcrop-now in compromised light
walking into the break room, mischievous eyes
                              meeting mine

   "George, George, what's it say"

   ■

The crow shadow
entering like a crow

in ways only
proximate—a moving
silhouette

though the sound
seems real enough—
a high pipe holler—

in like relations

to this rebus,
held to world by

a few cords and
strings, a few
fluids, muscles, and the
electrical mystery.

The shadow doesn't
fly, I change before
it does, then

I hear the caw
recede as it I imagine

changes to a scan.

■

Light being the thing
to which supplications are made

the smudge, the blur brings the rain down,
the reflection striates on the surface . . .

a viewpoint not a vision,
a town called Wide Ruin.

Rectitude spelled by fence and spire.

A stare comes from planes in his face.

■

Mill town, stack
and smoke at four
just east

squares of the
mountain burned
The work day's start

A rainbow curtain
separating the cloud
cover from the throng

contingent to the
overflow like a
contingency plan, "our

interest to maintain
relations with
the mainland,"

invert the terms
of service, denatured
explanations

through a microphone
as the crowd
stands, listens

though some hearing
it through soft bullets
in their ears

Cane stalk ash
trespasses, drifts
over the tourists

■

Waiting
        in
-volving

the orange
changing.

Harmony a
                low
order of

strength,
"before"

evening as
                in
standing

before it.
Then fold

your love
                in,
under

unstable,
sounded night.

My garden,
born from a scald.

Copper patch on
back. As if dorsal-
thrown. Black hairs

from the stun of
first immersion.

I come and tend

after the prone fires,
putting on another

coating of chrysalis.

■

To let the case
travel by neglect

"a common parent"

"a submerged chain"

"a body being invisible from
its velocity"

the import that appears
as scrub or wrack

at the wide morning
by lake water

people walking
their range

An old one writes, claims
a rock table

■

Down the press of long stairs
down step become level
to the immaterial

at the lighthouse form
of cold pure local
sun just slight outside
the graybright

just below the top-
most in a cling

and think to continue
when the real is not

with the known lengths

but what is is
and I vehicle.

■

Flew or present
already   birds

in the noise on the ground
they were flight noise

above various tongues
that were sitters on benches

vacant ones curled into phones
or open-lapped with their others

the random summer square
festive merely afternoon

as bird-sound heightened
and a pinecone fell

world-language in the not
so immaculately heard

and I thinking of the
large man his every day

suit and tie, his sentence
The attack is not the note.

They blow up strips of the geoplast and take things, coal, and crush things, gravel. They do this during the long nights and hooked together so that it is an endless night. When they look at one another it is the application. Off to the side of town in the downswing zone. They have lights apart to see the arm. Height limits to prevent the auspicious, colors of the resistances learned by racist mnemonics.

Products say to do that.

The rock moved to get to here, it became us.

A lifeline a steep way down and through—the mass you connect with implements. Might as well be spade and claw. He scoots toward the generator, a mile they later calculated, below wife and house. Question the expense of person equipped to force that procession along, rating scales of blind and numerous as the unit necessities get lived under a segmented carbon moon.

He touched it. Blue powder came out his knee

■

Then: built the location: then: they left. Building was the pact, populating would have to do with others. There were low divisions, shaken quickly from someone's utility-grade sleeve, large picture windows still bearing tape and grease-pencil signs of first delivery, making the structures hard to heat, swirled plaster for bark, set into dune landscapes which shared the debut with blowing coast, sun beating down, salt air, the hover of offshore squalls. In such place-building is crude entrance—whittled out of moment's matter into soonest shape. Mortars settling around the baited stillpoint of development, this simply is, might never become, the target market may be but marker.

tracks in the sand merge into sand

A ghost town in reverse

What is the history of a verb? faltering when parallel lines stop being parallel, or the anticipation between cloudbursts, distracted biped walking out of the forest. Wheel-spokes to smooth out the "in time" of the roll. Sensing rain or the end of rain. With plots to move, compress, exhume, preludes to the music of *ever after,* a hard social playback of the brightly lit.

Then: they build lights and medians to wait for the highway.

■

That bend a true bend
with stars out

In blackness it
seems to be
straight

With gray mist
you just have
to know

Discriminate
bluff reef (don't
steer into it)
and wind reef
(it isn't there)

Much would come
gauging the depth
to grade a hazard

And song from the bank
may be
adventure, irresistible
packet.

■

Chordal
hiss of making-
machines

is the mercantile
world working.
I attend

traces of internal
climates be-
cause

I'm caught on something.
The interruption
converted

a "train" I'd forgotten.
Something stand-
ing for the

noon

bell.

Not to give the address of the bomb

but one address a house

a town away.

No mouth, only
a deadline. The
tacit
confederates

Clubs for spouses,
swingsets
for the children

New world for the next
turns out to be a fever.

Backs straight,
facing
the solution-
event

Like the land itself regarding
what it means to be still

they watched it go up

he remembers the Gita.

The one moving scarce
to field the
accumulation.

A succession of city blocks

Project unfolding only
as it leaks
into the walk

Sounds of the phenomena,
the long and short

He says, not
a dynamic but a
straying—

Notice the intersections

Notice the pedestrians

He would carve his state—
the resonance merging
with its being
struck

onto a
grain.

■

Why do the energies
decide to surround

those words on that day
when they might abandon

them another. What fossil
has been made local.

A bloom creeps away,
becomes native. Will and

confusion in the
admixture, the measured

lines in a voice someone
left at the pass.

"I am tempted to say
the accident is shifting."

■

The copula on stilts
a day from eden

stilting above the den

■

Streeth,
slowth,
strangely the armor

let down for a few days
as with newborn
trying eyes

felt the non-armor's
realism.

The clouds form
to ribs and inch
east in a pallid
high renouncing

Then left with the pave
of yourself,

and a dark looking
deep until
at the deepest

decision
sensorium

begins the
speckle.

Movement of honey down a wall,
because like the sun after

contact with the hill

behind which it moves down

and that you can watch it, it's time

or that described as "sliding
behind"
in a brief to witness that
correspondence, honey/time

sun-hill/time   what it is

when into which   so a furrow
or fatedness might be uncovered

A vague plain billboard beside the mission
to hang the chronic messages on

■

Ocean bed in the open air,
ice   magnetism

where the continent sloughs
A skin in the re-telling
launched without notice,

a pencil rolling forward

Man migrated to watcher
as his hold dropped

Example not symbol
in the sustaining hemispheres,

the uneven cauldron of all signs,
even the arrows: mystery.

A speech-act in the ladle's
abrupt upbringing   folded leaf
the pure city at one end,
filled city the opposite,

what it means   what it does
to set one's stake
into the loosening fiber

alive   somewhere above the X.

◾

I walked over
there

because of the
prior

thought.
Later I

realized the
priority had

converted.
This in

a day of
occluded

promise—intensive
edges folded

back. But
looking for them

—as if to paste
an over-

drawn legend to
the wall—

like taking
your arms

with mine
around you,

the tactile
labyrinth

in a conditional
age of silver—

felt, it
felt, like

creation.

NIGHTBOAT BOOKS

Nightboat Books, a nonprofit organization, seeks to develop audiences for writers whose work resists convention and transcends boundaries. We publish books rich with poignancy, intelligence, and risk. Please visit our website, www.nightboat.org, to learn about our titles and how you can support our future publications.

This book was made possible by grants from The Fund for Poetry and the Topanga Fund, which is dedicated to promoting the arts and literature of California.

The following individuals have supported the publication of this book. We thank them for their generosity and commitment to the mission of Nightboat Books:

Kazim Ali
Elizabeth Motika
Benjamin Taylor

In addition, this book has been made possible, in part, by a grant from the New York State Council on the Arts Literature Program.

State of the Arts

NYSCA